A GIFT FOR:

_____

FROM:

_____

 ZONDERVAN®

Keeping Company with God
Copyright © 2007 by Philip D. Yancey

Requests for information should be addressed to:
Zondervan, *Grand Rapids, Michigan* 49530

ISBN-10: 0-310-81742-0
ISBN-13: 978-0-310-81742-0

Compiler: *Kathryn Helmers*
Product Manager: *Kim Zeilstra*
Production Manager: *Bev Stout*
Interior design: *Michael J. Williams*

Printed in China

07 08 09 10 11 12 13 • 23 22 21 20 19 18 17 16 15 14 13 12 11 10 9 8 7 6 5 4 3 2

PHILIP YANCEY

KEEPING COMPANY WITH GOD

A Prayer Journal

ZONDERVAN®

ZONDERVAN.com/
AUTHORTRACKER
follow your favorite authors

PREFACE

Books about prayer work somewhat like trail maps: they merely give you directions, leaving to you the hard work of taking the journey. Oddly enough, I have found that reading a book about prayer may feel more satisfying than praying, perhaps as reading a fitness magazine may feel more satisfying—and involve far less effort—than actually attempting the exercise regimen. In both cases, though, what matters most is what you *do*, not what you read.

I did not write the book *Prayer: Does It Make Any Difference?* as a sterile intellectual exercise. I sincerely hope that what I have learned translates into actual differences in my prayer life, and perhaps in yours.

This companion journal is designed to be a kind of travel journal for your adventures in prayer. Use it as a place to record your questions and thoughts along the way, your frustrations as well as your satisfactions. There is no right or wrong way to use it. If it helps in any way to make prayer a greater reality in your life, then I'm grateful, especially if it leads you into praying rather than simply reading about it.

The optional readings refer to relevant passages in *Prayer: Does It Make Any Difference?* If you have read that book you may recognize some of the words and thoughts in this journal. A superb editor, Kathy Helmers, mined some brief, appropriate passages that we hope may stimulate your own experience of prayer. This journal follows the general structure of my book on prayer, yet we designed the journal so that it would also be useful to someone who has not read the book, and there is much new supplemental material in it as well.

I have described prayer as a way of keeping company with God. Just as we have a variety of ways of keeping company with family and friends, friendship with God involves varied communication styles and levels of intimacy. As many people have found, a journal can help foster an ongoing conversation with God by providing a record of the times of closeness as well as the times of distance. Write in it when you pray and when you don't; when you remember God and when you forget God; when your heart seems full or when your words seem empty. As the prayers in the Bible make clear, God is big enough to encompass the messiness and sprawl of life. Indeed, in some mysterious way, God hungers for our attention.

My primary qualification for writing a book on prayer was that I felt unqualified but wanted to learn. I was surprised to find that the process of writing a book, which comprises a series of discrete tasks, actually helped make prayer a more natural practice for me. I asked people about their experiences with prayer. I thought about prayer at odd hours of the day and night. I made it more of a priority, and as a result prayer has become more integrated (a word with a Latin root meaning "undivided" or "whole") with the rest of my life.

I hope my musings about prayer help you to make prayer a more natural practice in your life, too — a way of keeping company with God that will prove healthy and beneficial no matter what you face in life.

Philip Yancey

CONNECTING

How does prayer work? What actual difference does it make in the "real" world? Why pray if God already knows what we're going to ask? Why ask if God has already determined the outcome?

These are the kinds of questions that have shaped my own struggles with prayer. No doubt you have your own list of questions. I have yet to meet someone honestly seeking to follow God who does *not* wrestle with prayer.

Sometimes, our questions keep us from praying. Other times, they hover in our thoughts while we're trying to pray, as if to mock our efforts. In the book *Prayer: Does It Make Any Difference?* I tried to face such restlessness head on, pressing into it rather than avoiding it. By a journalistic instinct, I pursue questions by researching, observing, interviewing others, and then processing what I have learned. As I searched the Bible and devotional classics, plumbed my own experiences of prayer, and explored others', insights began to emerge. Some led me toward answers even as others led to new ways of asking the questions.

In the process, my attitude toward prayer began to change. I used to view prayer as a duty; after all, seminaries cover the subject under the umbrella of "spiritual disciplines." In truth, most of us don't like discipline. I saw that I had viewed prayer much like calisthenics, something I really ought to do, out of a sense of obligation. I even had the immature notion that the more time and effort I put into prayer, the more attentively God would listen. I no longer see prayer as a kind of obligation. Indeed, I wonder if we should stop labeling prayer as a spiritual *discipline* and see it as a spiritual *privilege*. God has given us the enormous privilege of communicating, in a way that benefits us wholly. My life flourishes as I pray; I neglect the practice to my own detriment.

Prayer is a primary means of knowing God—and as such, it has features in common with all relationships that matter. It includes moments of ecstasy as well as dullness, mindless distraction and acute concentration, flashes of joy and bouts of irritation. It is the place where God and human beings meet. Where God and you can meet.

As you begin this journey into new ways of meeting with God, take some time to reflect on your past experiences with prayer. What kinds of expectations do you bring to this journey—for example, desires for what might occur, past frustrations you'd like to overcome, changes you hope to begin now and carry into the future? Listing them now will help establish a benchmark to which you can refer as you move through the pages ahead. What desires for and frustrations with prayer do you have in this season of your spiritual life?

_____

_____

_____

_____

_____

_____

_____

_____

_____

_____

_____

_____

_____

_____

_____

_____

_____

_____

_____

(Optional Reading: Chapter 3 opening through "Guilty," pages 30–33)

My soul thirsts for God, for the living God.
    When can I go and meet with God?
My tears have been my food
    day and night,
while men say to me all day long,
    "Where is your God?"
Why are you downcast, O my soul?
    Why so disturbed within me?
Put your hope in God,
    for I will yet praise him,
    my Savior and my God.

Psalm 42:2–3, 5–6

If you were composing a psalm about meeting God in prayer, what kinds of honest thoughts and feelings would you include? You need not compose formal poetry, but try addressing God directly about your current spiritual state.

_____

_____

_____

_____

_____

_____

_____

_____

_____

_____

_____

_____

_____

(Optional Reading: Chapter 1 opening through "A Universal Cry," pages 11–14)

n prayer I speak haltingly at first, "slow of speech and tongue" like Moses.
open my soul, exposing by will what God already knows by wisdom. The
psalms tell of panting with an open mouth, of thirsting for the living God, of
longing for God as parched earth longs for water. They sound like letters from
a heartsick lover, and at the core that's what we seekers are.

Think about your own spiritual path. Have there been times when you felt
an especially intense longing or heartfelt desire for God? Can you point to
anything that may have prompted those feelings?

> WHEN I PRAY, I HAVE
> NOTHING TO OFFER GOD
> EXCEPT MY ADMISSION
> THAT I DESPERATELY LONG
> FOR GOD TO RECEIVE ME IN
> MERCY AND LOVE.

In the same way, the Spirit helps us in our weakness. We do not know what we ought to pray for, but the Spirit himself intercedes for us with groans that words cannot express. And he who searches our hearts knows the mind of the Spirit, because the Spirit intercedes for the saints in accordance with God's will

Romans 8:26–27

Have you faced confusing situations when you did not know how or what to pray? How does Paul's teaching about the Holy Spirit shape your thinking about such times?

_____

_____

_____

_____

_____

_____

_____

_____

_____

_____

_____

_____

_____

_____

_____

_____

_____

_____

Are there ways of weaving prayer into your life that you have found particularly satisfying in the past?

_____

_____

_____

_____

_____

_____

_____

> WE CAN INVITE GOD INTO OUR LIVES AND OURSELVES INTO GOD'S. WHEN WE DO THAT, PUTTING OURSELVES ON A PERSONAL FOOTING WITH GOD, SO TO SPEAK, RELATIONSHIP HEATS UP AND A POTENTIAL FOR EXTRAORDINARY FRIENDSHIP STIRS TO LIFE. FOR GOD IS A PERSON, TOO, AND THOUGH A PERSON UNLIKE OURSELVES, ONE WHO SURELY FULFILLS MORE OF WHAT THAT WORD MEANS, NOT LESS.

_____

_____

_____

_____

_____

After rejecting the faith I was taught in my youth, I came back to God due to thanksgiving. Softened by such common graces as the beauties of nature, classical music, and romantic love, I realized my own harsh notions of God were misconceptions garnered from a church that had sorely missed the message of grace. "[Dante] Rossetti makes the remark somewhere, bitterly but with great truth," wrote G. K. Chesterton, "that the worst moment for an atheist is when he is really thankful and has nobody to thank."*

What moments can you recall when you felt a deep sense of gratitude? Did it give you a longing for Someone to thank?

_____

_____

_____

_____

_____

_____

_____

_____

_____

_____

_____

_____

_____

_____

_____

_____

_____

_____

*G. K. Chesterton, *Saint Francis of Assisi* (New York: Doubleday/Image, 1924), p. 78.

Artists will often speak of the creative experience as something transcendent that happens through them, not something they can control at will. They create great art by giving themselves to beauty, or truth, out of their love for it—not as something to manipulate and exploit in order to earn money or achieve fame. They hope to wring something creative out of the medium, rather than have the medium serve them. In the same way, those who seek God "lose themselves" in the process.

Have you ever had the sense of "losing yourself" while doing something you love—such as an outdoor activity, listening to music, making a meal for friends, or creating something artistic? How could such experiences become a form of prayer for you?

_____

_____

_____

_____

_____

_____

_____

_____

_____

_____

_____

_____

_____

_____

_____

> By bringing us into the presence of God, and giving us a glimpse of the view from above, prayer radically changes how we experience life.

_____

_____

_____

_____

How lovely is your dwelling place,
    O Lord Almighty!
My soul yearns, even faints,
    for the court of the Lord;
my heart and my flesh cry out
    for the living God.
Even the sparrow has found a home,
    and the swallow a nest for herself,
    where she may have her young—
a place near your altar,
    O Lord Almighty, My King and my God.
Blessed are those who dwell in your house;
    they are ever praising you.

                        Psalm 84:1–4

Read this passage aloud, slowly and thoughtfully. Take some time to let it sink down into your mind and heart. What words or images linger with you?

_____

_____

_____

_____

_____

_____

_____

_____

_____

_____

_____

_____

(Optional Reading: "Doing It Right" and "Prayer and Personality," pages 188–192)

My prayers falter, of course. Sometimes I feel at a loss, and must turn to Psalms or a book of prayers written by others, simply asking God to make them my prayers, because I have no words of my own. Jesus himself prayed the words of psalms in times of stress.

Many ways of prayer don't require us to come up with our own words — listening to or making music, meditative times in nature, periods of reflective silence, reading devotional writings, bodily expressions of worship, or any activity that focuses mind and heart on God. Often, such alternatives reflect the way we are "wired" as individuals. What fits for you, when you are longing to reach out to God but find yourself at a loss for words?

_____

_____

_____

_____

_____

_____

_____

_____

_____

_____

_____

_____

> THE MAIN PURPOSE OF PRAYER
> IS NOT TO MAKE LIFE EASIER,
> NOR TO GAIN MAGICAL POWERS,
> BUT TO KNOW GOD.

_____

_____

_____

_____

Write about some of your most significant experiences with prayer, positive or negative, past or present. They could be major or minor moments, times of frustration or deep gladness, feelings of closeness to God or lonely distance from God.

PRAYER ENCOMPASSES THE EPIPHANIES THAT HAPPEN DURING MY DAY: TURNING A CORNER ON A SKI TRAIL AND SEEING A GRAY FOX SKITTER AWAY, WATCHING THE PINK ALPENGLOW ON THE MOUNTAINS AS THE SUN SETS, MEETING AN OLD FRIEND AT THE GROCERY STORE. BY INCORPORATING THOSE EXPERIENCES INTO MY PRAYERS, I PROLONG AND SAVOR THEM SO THAT THEY DO NOT FALL TOO QUICKLY INTO MY MEMORY BANK, OR OUT OF IT.

Prayer humbles me. It reminds me of my own puny place in the universe, a solitary figure on a dot of a planet spinning around one star of billions. I cannot even comprehend the universe, much less contemplate running it (this was God's lesson to Job, another disappointed pray-er). In prayer, I present requests to a God I choose to trust despite the conditions on this planet that have caused God's graced favorites and God's own Son to tremble in fear and confusion. I trust the unfathomable equilibrium of God's power and God's wisdom, of omnipotence and omniscience.

Have you experienced times when you were able to see your own circumstances as one small part of a much bigger picture? How do you think prayer can be a gateway to this kind of "big picture" perspective?

As he taught, Jesus said, "Watch out for the teachers of the law. They like to walk around in flowing robes and be greeted in the marketplaces, and have the most important seats in the synagogues and the places of honor at banquets. They devour widows' houses and for a show make lengthy prayers. Such men will be punished most severely."

Mark 12:38–40

Why do you think Jesus warned against these "teachers of the law" so sternly? What modern parallels come to mind?

_____

_____

_____

_____

_____

> APPARENTLY GOD IS THE
> KIND OF FRIEND WHO
> REWARDS HONESTY.

_____

_____

_____

_____

_____

_____

_____

_____

_____

_____

_____

_____

_____

_____

When I wrote about prayer I began with us, the pray-ers, rather than God, the one to whom we pray, because so many of us who pray come to the work awkwardly, self-consciously, as raw beginners. In attempting this strange act, we think of ourselves more than we think of God.

Do you ever feel as if you get in your own way when you're trying to pray? What keeps you from being authentic and vulnerable—naked—before God?

Prayer was, for Jesus, a link to the Father and the place of his true identity. One of his disciples, John, would later get a glimpse of that true state: " ... his eyes were like blazing fire.... In his right hand he held seven stars.... His face was like the sun shining in all its brilliance" (Revelation 1:14–16).

We can see a very different picture in Isaiah's prophecy, recorded centuries earlier, depicting the Messiah's earthly life:

He had no beauty or majesty to attract us to him,
    nothing in his appearance that we should desire him.
He was despised and rejected by men,
    a man of sorrows, and familiar with suffering.
Like one from whom men hide their faces
    he was despised, and we esteemed him not.

Isaiah 53:2–3

List some of the differences you see in these two contrasting pictures of Jesus. What does this list suggest to you about why prayer was so important to Jesus in his life on earth? And how can prayer play a similar role in reminding you of the "unseen world?"

_____

_____

_____

_____

_____

_____

_____

_____

_____

_____

_____

What are some of your *most* satisfying experiences with prayer? What made them so satisfying?

_____

_____

_____

_____

_____

_____

_____

_____

_____

_____

_____

_____

_____

_____

_____

> MYSTERY, AWARENESS OF ANOTHER WORLD, AN EMPHASIS ON BEING RATHER THAN DOING, EVEN A FEW MOMENTS OF QUIET DO NOT COME NATURALLY TO ME IN THIS HECTIC, BUZZING WORLD. I MUST CARVE OUT TIME AND ALLOW GOD TO NOURISH MY INNER LIFE.

_____

_____

_____

_____

Now faith is being sure of what we hope for and certain of what we do not see.

Hebrews 11:1

Read this verse aloud, at least twice. People have varying kinds of faith, from simple childlike faith to a hang-on-by-the-fingernails fidelity. How would you describe your own faith? Has it changed over the years?

_____

_____

_____

_____

_____

_____

_____

_____

_____

_____

_____

_____

_____

_____

_____

_____

_____

_____

_____

_____

The word *company*, as in "keeping company with God," simply means "with bread," and comes from the ancient and universal tradition of hospitality. We connect with others by inviting them into our homes, by breaking bread and sharing everyday life.

Take some time to reflect on what is working and what isn't in your efforts to "keep company" with God. How can you invite God into your life, and yourself into God's? Write in the form of a prayer, if you'd like.

> I PRAY IN HOPES OF DISCERNING WHAT GOD WANTS, AND IN HOPES OF BRINGING MY OWN DESIRES IN LINE WITH GOD'S.

(Optional Reading: "Honest," pages 40–42)

Prayer is a subversive act performed in a world that constantly calls faith into question. I may have a sense of estrangement in the very act of prayer, yet by faith I continue to pray and to look for other signs of God's presence.... I have learned to see prayer not as my way of establishing God's presence, rather as a way of responding to God's presence that is a fact whether I can detect it or not

How do you react when your doubts make it difficult to pray? Mention specific times, if you can.

_____

_____

_____

_____

_____

_____

_____

> WHY DOES PRAYER RANK
> SO HIGH ON SURVEYS OF
> THEORETICAL IMPORTANCE
> AND SO LOW ON SURVEYS OF
> ACTUAL SATISFACTION?

_____

_____

_____

_____

_____

_____

_____

_____

_____

Since we have a great high priest who has gone through the heavens, Jesus the Son of God, let us hold firmly to the faith we profess. For we do not have a high priest who is unable to sympathize with our weaknesses, but we have one who has been tempted in every way, just as we are—yet was without sin. Let us then approach the throne of grace with confidence, so that we may receive mercy and find grace to help us in our time of need.

Hebrews 4:14–16

What are some weaknesses in your own life, for which you need Christ's mercy and grace?

_____

_____

_____

_____

_____

_____

_____

_____

_____

_____

_____

_____

_____

_____

_____

_____

_____

_____

Mention some experiences with prayer that remain disappointing or frustrating to you.

_____

_____

_____

_____

_____

_____

_____

_____

_____

_____

_____

_____

_____

> THE PSALMS READ LIKE
> UNINHIBITED PRIVATE MEMOS
> TO THE MAJOR PARTNER.
> (THE PROPHETS GIVE GOD'S
> SIDE OF THE EQUATION.) GOD
> FORMED AN ALLIANCE BASED
> ON THE WORLD AS IT IS, FULL
> OF FLAWS, WHEREAS PRAYER
> CALLS GOD TO ACCOUNT FOR
> THE WORLD AS IT SHOULD BE.

esus freely admitted his dependence: "the Son can do nothing by himself; he can do only what he sees his Father doing" (John 5:19). In a telling comment Jesus also said, "Your Father knows what you need before you ask him" Matthew 6:8). He could not mean that prayer is unnecessary, for his own life relied that. He could only mean that we need not strive to convince God to are; the Father already cares, more than we can know. Prayer is not a matter of giving God new information.

How would you finish this sentence? "Prayer is not a matter of giving God information about our needs. Instead, prayer is _____."

_____

_____

_____

_____

_____

_____

_____

_____

_____

_____

_____

_____

_____

_____

_____

_____

_____

_____

(Optional Reading: "Jesus at Prayer," pages 77–79)

Jesus valued prayer enough to spend many hours at the task. If I had to answer the question "Why pray?" in one sentence, it would be, "Because Jesus did." He bridged the chasm between God and human beings. While on earth he became vulnerable, as we are vulnerable; rejected, as we are rejected; and tested, as we are tested. In every case his response was prayer.

Think of a time recently when you felt life pressing in on you. How did you respond—panic, anxiety, resentment, wishing you could make it all just go away? Do you believe prayer can make any difference for you in times like this?

Most of my struggles in the Christian life circle around the same two themes: why God doesn't act the way we want God to, and why I don't act the way God wants me to. Prayer is the precise point where those themes converge.

What tends to affect your sense of connecting with God, either positively or negatively? Does prayer have any part in that process?

_____

_____

_____

_____

_____

_____

_____

_____

_____

> DEEP DOWN I BELIEVED THAT CONTACT WITH GOD SHOULD BE FULFILLING AND EVEN TRANSFORMING, YET I RARELY FOUND IT SO. I ASSUMED I MUST BE DOING SOMETHING WRONG.

_____

_____

_____

_____

_____

_____

WRESTLING

The Bible gives us a record of God's desire for relationship with human beings. From beginning to end, it underscores the theme of God seeking companionship with us. The opening chapters of Genesis picture God conversing with the first two human beings in the unspoiled beauty of their primeval garden. The closing chapters of Revelation unveil God's plan for dwelling forever with the human race, redeemed and restored. If I had to summarize the story of the Bible in one sentence, it would be "God gets his family back."

Yet we live between Genesis and Revelation, an interlude during which the polluted atmosphere of a rebellious planet disrupts perfect communication. "Your will be done on earth as it is in heaven," Jesus taught us to pray, clearly implying that God's will is *not* being done that way on earth. As a result, in a fallen world that constantly pulls us away from God or even calls God into question, prayer may seem more like a wrestling match than casual conversation. Most surprisingly, God invites the scuffle.

I have recounted a story from the church I attend, which reserves a brief time for people in the pews to voice aloud their prayers. Over the years I have heard hundreds of these prayers, and with very few exceptions the word *polite* applies. One, however, stands out in my memory because of its raw emotion.

In a clear but wavering voice a young woman began with the words, "God, I hated you after the rape! How could you let this happen to me?" The congregation abruptly fell silent. No more rustling of papers or shifting in the seats. "And I hated the people in this church who tried to comfort me. I didn't want comfort. I wanted revenge. I wanted to hurt back. I thank you, God, that you didn't give up on me, and neither did some of these people. You kept after me, and I come back to you now and ask that you heal the scars in my soul."

Although that was one of the most unusual prayers I have heard in church, it would fit right in with the prayers I find in the Bible. Most of us have learned to domesticate our prayers, to make them "acceptable," but God seems to want something more reflective of our true feelings, however unacceptable they may seem by other standards. Perhaps God values our questions more than we do.

Have you ever tried expressing your most painful feelings and questions to God in prayer—perhaps not publicly, as this woman did, but privately, just between you and God?

(Optional Reading: "A Threat to Faith," pages 216–220)

I am worn out calling for help;
   my throat is parched.
My eyes fail,
   looking for my God.

                    Psalm 69:3

How do you think most people feel about expressing anger and disappointment with God in prayer? Jot down some prayers you have heard that stand out in memory.

_____

_____

_____

_____

_____

_____

_____

_____

_____

_____

_____

_____

_____

_____

_____

_____

_____

_____

_____

Whoever wrestles with God in prayer risks the possibility that the God who an answer will simply remain silent.

Think of a time when you found yourself confronting God's apparent silence regarding a request. How did you respond?

> IN PRAYER WE STAND BEFORE GOD
> TO PLEAD OUR CONDITION AS WELL
> AS THE CONDITIONS AROUND US. IN
> THE PROCESS, THE ACT OF PRAYER
> EMBOLDENS ME TO JOIN THE WORK OF
> TRANSFORMING THE WORLD INTO A
> PLACE WHERE THE FATHER'S WILL IS
> INDEED DONE AS IT IS IN HEAVEN.

When alone, Jesus relied on prayer as a kind of spiritual recharging. After an exhausting day of ministry—recruiting disciples, preaching to crowds, healing the sick—he would withdraw to an isolated place to pray.... "I have food to eat that you know nothing about" (John 4:32), he reassured his disciples, who worried about his lack of nourishment at such times.

Can you think of times when prayer actually helped sustain or nourish you during difficulties?

_____

_____

_____

_____

_____

_____

_____

IF GOD WANTS INTIMACY WITH US, WHY MUST WE GO THROUGH DESERT EXPERIENCES WHERE GOD REMAINS SILENT AND DISTANT?	_____

_____

_____

_____

_____

_____

_____

acob was left alone, and a man wrestled with him till daybreak. When the man saw that he could not overpower him, he touched the socket of Jacob's hip so that his hip was wrenched as he wrestled with the man. Then the man said, "Let me go, for it is daybreak."

But Jacob replied, "I will not let you go unless you bless me."

The man asked him, "What is your name?"

"Jacob," he answered.

Then the man said, "Your name will no longer be Jacob but Israel [lit. "he struggles with God"], because you have struggled with God and with men and have overcome."

Genesis 32:24–28

How do you tend to respond to people who "wrestle" or contend with you? Does it surprise you that God affirmed, rather than scolded, Jacob? What does that tell you about God?

Have you ever had an experience of "wrestling" with God in prayer? What was the result?

_____

_____

_____

_____

_____

_____

THE CARPENTER, WHEN
HE GLUES TOGETHER TWO
BOARDS, KEEPS THEM
TIGHTLY CLAMPED TILL
THE CEMENT SETS, AND
THE OUTWARD PRESSURE IS
NO MORE NEEDED; THEN HE
UNSCREWS. SO WITH THE
CALAMITIES, DEPRESSIONS,
AND DISAPPOINTMENTS
THAT CRUSH US INTO CLOSE
CONTACT WITH GOD.

_____

_____

_____

_____

_____

_____

_____

_____

_____

_____

_____

_____

_____

For most of us, prayer serves as a resource to help in a time of testing or conflict. For Jesus, it was the battle itself. Once the Gethsemane prayers had aligned him with the Father's will, what happened next was merely the means to fulfill it.

When you are facing a difficult challenge, are you more likely or less likely to turn to God in prayer, and why?

_____

_____

_____

_____

_____

_____

_____

_____

_____

_____

_____

_____

_____

_____

_____

_____

_____

_____

_____

_____

(Optional Reading: "Making Requests Known," pages 143–144)

A true partner, God has given us the right to speak to everything that concerns us. Not to do so, in fact, endangers the very intimacy God desires.

Make a list of some things you have recently spoken to God about in prayer. Are there significant areas of your life that you notice are missing from this list?

_____

_____

_____

_____

_____

_____

_____

_____

_____

IN A PARADOX THAT I KEEP FORGETTING, GOD NEEDS MY CONFESSED WEAKNESS FAR MORE THAN MY STRENGTH.	_____
	_____
	_____
	_____
	_____

_____

_____

_____

_____

_____

(Optional Reading: "Stages of Prayer," pages 106–109)

Jesus went with his disciples to a place called Gethsemane, and he said to them, "Sit here while I go over there and pray." He took Peter and the two sons of Zebedee along with him, and he began to be sorrowful and troubled. Then he said to them, "My soul is overwhelmed with sorrow to the point of death. Stay here and keep watch with me."

Going a little farther, he fell with his face to the ground and prayed, "My Father, if it is possible, may this cup be taken from me. Yet not as I will, but as you will."

Matthew 26:36–39

Read this passage slowly and thoughtfully, allowing it to sink down into your mind and heart. What words or images stand out to you? In your own words, how would you describe the struggle that Jesus faced?

_____

_____

_____

_____

_____

_____

_____

_____

_____

_____

_____

_____

_____

_____

_____

_____

_____

(Optional Reading: "Once Is Not Enough," pages 150–153)

The apostle Paul, who had healed others, pleaded in vain for the removal of his thorn in the flesh. Paul learned that his opportunity for grace would come not in divine healing but in the more difficult path of acceptance. Paul's attitude, his expectations, his emphasis in prayer, and perhaps even his theology made a sudden shift: "Therefore I will boast all the more gladly about my weaknesses, so that Christ's power may rest on me. That is why, for Christ's sake, I delight in weaknesses, in insults, in hardships, in persecutions, in difficulties. For when I am weak, then I am strong" (1 Corinthians 12:9–10).

It is more common to deny or feel ashamed of weakness than to "boast" in it. Have you ever experienced relief in bringing a weakness to God in prayer?

Are there specific circumstances or feelings that you have trouble praying about? Simply naming them could be a form of praying about them.

_____

_____

_____

_____

_____

_____

_____

_____

_____

_____

_____

_____

_____

_____

_____

_____

> UNLESS I CAN SOMEHOW GAIN THE HUMILITY TO FACE WHO I AM, I WILL NEVER KNOW WHO GOD IS. WHEN I PRAY, I HAVE NOTHING TO OFFER GOD EXCEPT MY ADMISSION THAT I DESPERATELY LONG FOR GOD TO RECEIVE ME IN MERCY AND LOVE.

_____

_____

_____

_____

_____

_____

Almost a fifth of the verses in the Gospels deal with Jesus' healing ministry. That fact gives a bright clue into God's desire for all of us on planet earth. At no time did Jesus announce, "You just have to put up with it. This affliction is God's will for you." *Every* time, without exception, he healed whoever asked. For this reason alone, I could never say to a suffering person, "You must accep this as God's will," or "God has selected you to bear this particular pain." Jesu refuted the Pharisees who pronounced God's will in disasters (Luke 13) and his disciples who tried to locate God's will in a man's blindness (John 9).

Have you ever stopped praying about something because you figured that God's "will" had already dictated the outcome, which no amount of prayers could change? Can you think of any advantage to persisting in prayer even when the desired answer does not come?

_____

_____

_____

_____

_____

_____

_____

_____

_____

_____

_____

_____

_____

_____

_____

_____

uppose a brother or sister is without clothes and daily food. If one of you ays to him, "Go, I wish you well; keep warm and well fed," but does nothing bout his physical needs, what good is it? In the same way, faith by itself, if it s not accompanied by action, is dead.

James 2:15

ubstitute the words "I'll pray for you" instead of "Go, I wish you well." What aution does this verse give about prayer?

_____

_____

_____

_____

_____

_____

_____

_____

_____

> I ONCE ENVISIONED INTERCESSION AS BRINGING REQUESTS TO GOD THAT GOD MAY NOT HAVE THOUGHT OF, THEN TALKING GOD INTO GRANTING THEM. NOW I SEE INTERCESSION AS AN INCREASE IN *MY* AWARENESS.

(Optional Reading: "A Leap of Trust," pages 209–212)

I sat in the living room of Tim Hansel who, after a rock-climbing fall that crushed most of the vertebrae in his back, fights waves of pain that vary from excruciating to intolerable. Once a powerful outdoors adventurer, now he hunches over and has the tired, wrinkled face of a man much older. "Pain is part of the process," he says. Somehow he finds the strength to speak to groups whenever possible, reminding them of the precious gift of life. "I have prayed hundreds, if not thousands of times, for the Lord to heal me," Tim says, "and he finally healed me … of the need to be healed. The way one reacts to the suffering of life matters more than the suffering itself."

Do you know anyone in Tim Hansel's condition of long-term chronic pain? What would you suggest he or she pray for?

he term "wrestling" connotes engagement, an interaction between two individuals. Yet during dry times prayer can feel futile, like trying to have a conversation with someone who never responds, or who is not even there. In our experiences of prayer, describe a time when you *did* sense that God was "here" while you were praying. What seems to make the difference for you in experiencing prayer as a two-way interaction rather than as a one-way exercise?

> TALKING TO GOD COMES FROM GOD HIMSELF, FOR WE PRAY AS A RESPONSE TO WHAT GOD HAS ALREADY DONE IN THE WORLD AND IN OUR LIVES.

Be strong in the Lord and in his mighty power. Put on the full armor of God so that you can take your stand against the devil's schemes. For our struggle is not against flesh and blood, but against the rulers, against the authorities, against the powers of this dark world and against the spiritual forces of evil in the heavenly realms.

Ephesians 6:10–1

Have you ever sensed this spiritual struggle Paul describes in Ephesians? If so how did it affect the way you prayed?

_____

_____

_____

_____

_____

_____

> EVEN WHEN PRAYER
> SEEMS LIKE A DUTY, LIKE A
> HOMEWORK ASSIGNMENT,
> WE SUSTAIN THE HOPE
> THAT IT COULD GROW
> INTO SOMETHING MORE.

_____

_____

_____

_____

_____

_____

_____

_____

My initial word of advice on struggling with doubt is, *Don't panic.* I have yet to find a single shade of doubt not represented in the Bible's own accounts, which means that doubt will hardly surprise God.

Which of the following statements is more true to your experience?

"I take my doubt to God in prayer."

"Doubt tends to keep me from praying."

What tilts you toward one answer over the other?

_____

_____

_____

_____

_____

_____

_____

_____

_____

_____

_____

_____

_____

_____

_____

_____

_____

To paraphrase a British archbishop, "If you want to know what God is like, look at Jesus." The compassion Jesus showed toward those who requested help and healing gives a visible sign as to how God in heaven must hear our requests.

Write down any specific times you can remember of Jesus responding to requests for help and healing. To jog your memory, flip through some passages in the Gospels, looking for such stories.

_____

_____

_____

_____

_____

_____

_____

_____

_____

_____

_____

_____

_____

_____

_____

_____

_____

_____

_____

People were also bringing babies to Jesus to have him touch them. When the disciples saw this, they rebuked them. But Jesus called the children to him and said, "Let the little children come to me, and do not hinder them, for the kingdom of God belongs to such as these. I tell you the truth, anyone who will not receive the kingdom of God like a little child will never enter it."

Luke 18:15–17

Put yourself in the place of one of the children welcomed by Jesus. How do children present requests to adults? What does this teach you about prayer?

A HIDDEN TREASURE LIES INSIDE, IF ONLY WE CAN QUARRY IT. A NEW COUNTRY AWAITS US, IF ONLY WE CAN FIND THE LANGUAGE IN WHICH TO CONVERSE.

In any close relationship, it may be necessary from time to time to have a talk that "clears the air" of anything that has built up and is interfering with intimacy. What if you were to ask God for an "air-clearing" talk—what would be on your list of things to discuss, whether by way of confession, questioning, complaint, a need for forgiveness, or any other concerns?

_____

_____

_____

_____

_____

_____

_____

> I BRING MY REQUESTS TO
> GOD IN ORDER TO ALIGN
> THEM WITH GOD'S
> PURPOSES, RECOGNIZING
> PRAYER AS AN ACTIVE
> WAY OF REALIZING
> THOSE PURPOSES.

_____

_____

_____

_____

_____

_____

_____

_____

_____

_____

marvel at God's restraint, and the pain it must cause. When I sit with parents and hear their stories of children who make self-destructive choices, bringing pain into the whole family, I think what it must be like for God to see us do the same. An aggrieved parent gives the best glimpse of how God must view our self-destroying race. "We all like sheep have gone astray, each of us has turned to his own way; and the LORD has laid on him the iniquity of us all" (Isaiah 53:6).

Choose a concern or burden that you have been carrying—perhaps one you have prayed about several times. The next time you pray about it, try asking God to help you see this situation from his perspective. You might want to take at least a day, or more, to let this request linger before God, and to be attentive to possible responses that could come in a variety of ways. If and when you notice them, be sure to write them down so you won't forget them.

_____

_____

_____

_____

_____

_____

_____

_____

_____

_____

_____

_____

_____

_____

_____

_____

_____

(Optional Reading: "Joining the Stream," pages 23–24)

I don't want to miss the chance that God might influence the things and people I care most about. Intercessory prayer introduces a new stream of influence involving God, me, and the person I'm praying for.

Make a list of some of the things and people you care most about.

_____

_____

_____

_____

_____

_____

_____

_____

_____

_____

> I AM LEARNING TO DISMANTLE THE BARRIERS SEPARATING THE ACT OF PRAYER FROM THE REST OF LIFE AND INSTEAD TO INVITE GOD TO "IMPOSE" ON MY TIGHTLY ORDERED LIFE.

_____

_____

_____

_____

_____

_____

_____

Paradoxically, those who seemingly have most to be thankful for apparently are least likely to exercise that spirit. Living in a state bursting with national parks and wilderness areas, I cannot comprehend a trend that pollsters can verify: residents of two of this country's most beautiful states, Oregon and Washington, worship the least, and communities around national parks show less religious faith than, say, those who live in the rural South or the inner city.

North Americans who go on short-term mission trips to third-world countries often return with glowing reports about the fervency they have found among believers. Eager faith in the midst of poverty contrasts sharply with the complacency and self-centeredness back home in the land of plenty.

Where are your opportunities to participate in God's work in the world through prayer and action, expressing a grateful spirit by seeking to meet needs of those who are less fortunate than you? Think of individuals, families, or communities you might already be aware of, or are connected to in some way, to whom you can help show Christ's mercy and grace.

_____

_____

_____

_____

_____

_____

_____

_____

_____

_____

_____

_____

_____

_____

_____

CONVERSING

The idea of a finite, flesh-and-blood person "conversing" with an infinite, invisible God in prayer may seem far-fetched. Yet surveys show that most people have a kind of prayer reflex that gets triggered just as surely as a healthy person's leg kicks when a doctor taps on the knee with a rubber hammer. The writer Anne Lamott says her favorite prayers are "Thanks, thanks, thanks!" and "Help! Help! Help!"

Instinctively we turn to prayer when we feel grateful, because we know that the deepest joys — life, beauty, love — are not accomplishments earned, but gifts received. We rush to prayer when we feel afraid, because we know that we have no control over the frailty and uncertainty of life. In the wake of tragedy or injustice we shake our fists at heaven or bang on its doors, because we know that God alone has power to right the wrongs of life.

If we already have a prayer impulse wired into our spiritual psyches, so to speak, what makes it so difficult to converse with God when we intentionally set aside time to pray?

I have experienced times when prayer made little sense. Questions muzzled me — Why tell God what God already knows? Why ask God to be merciful if God is by nature merciful? Why pray at all? For a solid year I could come up with no authentic prayers of my own and simply read from prayers in a *Liturgy of the Hours,* asking God to take those written words and accept them as my prayers whether I felt them sincerely or not. Then one day the cloud lifted and I wondered what had been my problem all that time.

The impulse to pray might come naturally, but the fluency of talking easily with God does not. Sometimes it comes with practice; other times, it slips away for no apparent reason. As the language of a living relationship, we can expect it to flow and change. Prayer is not simply a skill to be acquired, but an intimacy to be pursued.

(Optional Reading: Chapter 12 opening, "Yearning for Fluency," pages 157–158)

When has it seemed easy for you to experience prayer as a form of "conversing" with God? When has it seemed hard?

_____

_____

_____

_____

_____

_____

_____

_____

_____

_____

_____

_____

_____

_____

_____

_____

_____

_____

_____

_____

_____

_____

_____

_____

_____

_____

(Optional Reading: "Friendship," pages 59–62)

The LORD would speak to Moses face to face, as a man speaks with his friend.

Exodus 33:11

Moses was unique among the Israelites in his intimacy with God. Would you describe your own relationship with God as "friendship"? If not, how would you describe it?

A VINTNER EXPLAINED
TO ME THAT HE REFUSES
TO IRRIGATE HIS VINES
BECAUSE THE STRESS
CAUSED BY OCCASIONAL
DROUGHT PRODUCES
THE BEST, MOST TASTY
GRAPES. SEASONS OF
DRYNESS MAKE THE
ROOTS RUN DEEP,
STRENGTHENING THE
VINE FOR WHATEVER
THE FUTURE HOLDS.

the scribes in Ireland, who copied manuscripts and illuminated them with striking illustrations, kept a kind of diary with God, often jotting in the margins of their manuscripts. Since many of them had taken a vow of silence, writing was their normal way of expression. Wrote one anonymous scribe: "I am very cold without fire or covering … the robin is singing gloriously, but though its red breast is beautiful I am all alone. Oh God be gracious to my soul and grant me a better handwriting." Reading those notes, I get the sense of a "natural" flow of communication with God.

Do you invite God into the natural rhythms of your life? What might that look like?

_____

_____

_____

_____

_____

_____

_____

_____

_____

_____

_____

_____

_____

_____

_____

_____

_____

_____

In Jesus' day you could actually strike up a friendship with the Son of God. You could camp out with him in the desert, quiz him on the meaning of his cryptic stories, ask for advice about family matters, join him for dinner at the home of a Pharisee or tax collector.

If you could choose to be part of one scene in Jesus' earthly life, what would it be, and why?

_____

_____

_____

_____

_____

_____

_____

_____

_____

_____

_____

_____

_____

_____

_____

_____

_____

_____

esus said, "You are my friends if you do what I command. I no longer call
ou servants, because a servant does not know his master's business. Instead,
have called you friends, for everything that I learned from my Father I have
ıade known to you."

John 15:14–15

Iow might it be possible to have a kind of "friendship" with Jesus now, simi-
ır to the way he described it to his disciples in this passage?

_____

_____

_____

_____

_____

_____

_____

_____

_____

_____

_____

_____

_____

_____

_____

> PRAYER INVITES GOD
> INTO MY WORLD AND
> USHERS ME INTO
> GOD'S.

_____

_____

_____

_____

_____

_____

We think of conversing as an exchange of words, but in an intimate friendship nonverbal ways of communicating contribute as well. Can you think of nonverbal ways of "conversing" with God?

_____

_____

_____

_____

_____

_____

_____

_____

THE BIBLE ITSELF INCLUDES A MULTITUDE OF STYLES. PETER KNELT, JEREMIAH STOOD, NEHEMIAH SAT DOWN, ABRAHAM PROSTRATED HIMSELF, AND ELIJAH PUT HIS FACE BETWEEN HIS KNEES. IN JESUS' DAY MOST JEWS STOOD, LIFTING THEIR OPEN EYES TO HEAVEN. THE VIRGIN MARY PRAYED IN POETRY; PAUL INTERSPERSED HIS PRAYERS WITH SINGING.

_____

_____

_____

_____

_____

_____

_____

_____

_____

_____

_____

_____

_____

_____

_____

_____

_____

He tends his flock like a shepherd:
   He gathers the lambs in his arms
and carries them close to his heart;
   he gently leads those that have young.
                              Isaiah 40:11

This tender imagery occurs amid descriptions of God's unearthly power. (You may want to read Isaiah 40 in context.) In your own prayers, do you imagine a God of great power or great tenderness? Is there a way to do both?

_____

_____

_____

_____

_____

_____

_____

_____

_____

_____

_____

_____

_____

_____

_____

_____

_____

_____

_____

_____

KEEPING COMPANY WITH GOD

(Optional Reading: Chapter 13 opening, "Prayer Grammar," pages 170–171)

We don't need to go through a formula and learn the proper steps for prayer. We can just pray, as a conversation, not a performance — the difference between talking to a friend and preparing a speech.

Prayers in the Bible, especially the Psalms, include both formal and informal types. Read Psalm 32 or 34, which include some of both styles. Reflect on your own prayers: Do you tend to treat prayer like a formal address to a critical audience or an intimate conversation with a friend?

et the peace of Christ rule in your hearts, since as members of one body you ere called to peace. And be thankful. Let the word of Christ dwell in you ichly as you teach and admonish one another with all wisdom, and as you ing psalms, hymns and spiritual songs with gratitude in your hearts to God. .nd whatever you do, whether in word or deed, do it all in the name of the .ord Jesus, giving thanks to God the Father through him.

Colossians 3:15 – 17

ead this passage slowly and thoughtfully, allowing it to sink down into your nind and heart. What words or images stand out to you?

WHAT IS FAITH, AFTER
ALL, BUT BELIEVING IN
ADVANCE WHAT WILL
ONLY MAKE SENSE IN
REVERSE?

In human relationships, I gradually learn what pleases each of my friends. When guests come for a visit, especially a repeat visit, I have a good idea what kind of restaurant they might enjoy, whether they would prefer to climb a mountain, ski down a slope, or sit by a fire. And the more time I spend with God, the more I learn what brings God pleasure.

List some of the things that might bring God pleasure. Now ask yourself, "What did I do today (or this week) that brought God pleasure?"

> PRAYER HELPS CORRECT MYOPIA, CALLING TO MIND A PERSPECTIVE I DAILY FORGET. I KEEP REVERSING ROLES, THINKING OF WAYS IN WHICH GOD SHOULD SERVE ME, RATHER THAN VICE VERSA.

Decide on a specific period of time, on a particular day in the coming week, that you can set aside for "conversing" with God, perhaps in a form that is a bit different for you. For example, you could write a brief letter to God, read it aloud, and then sit in silence for a while. You could choose a piece of music you love, and allow it to carry you to God in prayer. You may prefer to sit in silence at a favorite outdoor site, letting your heart speak for you instead of your head. Or you could simply light a candle, sit down at the kitchen table with a cup of coffee or tea, and talk to God as if you knew God were sitting across from you, waiting to hear about your life. If you want, write about it afterwards: what felt good, what felt awkward, what was disappointing, what was gratifying.

_____

_____

_____

_____

_____

_____

_____

_____

_____

_____

_____

_____

_____

_____

_____

_____

_____

_____

_____

_____

_____

_____

When prayer seems too much a burden, I compare it to what other religions require of their followers. Even in the Old Testament, worshipers had to raise crops and animals, then travel to a temple and present their offerings to priests in costly and bloody sacrifices. But when Jesus died, the thick curtain in the temple split from top to bottom, opening up direct access to God. In furthering a relationship with us, God primarily asks that we pray.

What does it say to you about God, that he places such high value on prayer?

_____

_____

_____

_____

_____

_____

_____

_____

_____

_____

_____

_____

_____

_____

_____

_____

_____

_____

esus said, "Peace I leave with you; my peace I give you. I do not give to you as
he world gives. Do not let your hearts be troubled and do not be afraid."

John 14:27

n what ways, if any, has prayer been a channel of God's peace for you?

_____

_____

_____

_____

_____

_____

_____

_____

_____

_____

_____

_____

_____

_____

_____

_____

_____

> FROM JESUS' LIFE ON
> EARTH I AM CONVINCED
> THAT GOD DESIRES FOR
> US HEALTH AND NOT
> SUFFERING.

_____

_____

_____

_____

_____

(Optional Reading: "Prayer Reminders," pages 181–183)

Some streams of Christian tradition emphasize fixed prayers or prayer rituals over conversational prayer. Catholic theologian Karl Rahner found himself praying the rosary as he sought to cling to his faith in the rubble of Munich a the end of a war. Dietrich Bonhoeffer, a Lutheran pastor sentenced to execution was surprised to find solace in making the sign of a cross.

Do you ever use fixed prayers, or physical "rituals," as a way of communicating with God in contrast to spontaneous, conversational prayer? If so, what kind of difference does it make for you?

_____

_____

_____

_____

_____

_____

_____

_____

_____

_____

_____

_____

_____

_____

_____

_____

_____

_____

The hundreds of prayers in the Bible offer a foundation for anyone seeking to improve the grammar and language of prayer. And as a reader becomes more acquainted with the Bible, even its stories and more obscure sections become a spur for prayers.

Other than Jesus' teaching of the Lord's Prayer, how do the words of the Bible shape the way you pray?

_____

_____

_____

_____

_____

_____

_____

_____

_____

_____

_____

_____

_____

> THAT PRAYER EXISTS AT ALL IS A GIFT OF GRACE, A GENEROUS INVITATION TO PARTICIPATE IN THE FUTURE OF THE COSMOS.

_____

_____

_____

_____

_____

_____

The Bible speaks in many places about silence, which is also included among the classic spiritual disciplines. Sometimes, observing silence in prayer can provide a way of cleansing our spiritual palate, or refreshing us when we return to using words. Try experimenting with a few minutes (or more) of silence across a few days or a week, to see if it affects the way you usually pray. What do you "hear" in silence?

_____

_____

_____

_____

_____

_____

_____

_____

_____

_____

_____

_____

_____

_____

_____

_____

_____

_____

_____

_____

_____

I wait for you, O LORD;
  you will answer, O Lord my God.
                     Psalm 38:15

Describe a particularly difficult area in your life, in which you have been
"forced" to wait on God. Can you pray about it with the words of the psalmist
in this verse?

_____

_____

_____

_____

_____

_____

_____

_____

_____

_____

_____

_____

_____

_____

_____

_____

_____

> WE DO NOT DETERMINE "GOD'S
> WILL" BY AGONIZING OVER PAIN
> AND WONDERING WHAT HIDDEN
> MESSAGE GOD MIGHT HAVE
> INTENDED. RATHER, WE ENTER
> INTO GOD'S WILL BY RESPONDING
> IN TRUST AND FAITH.

_____

_____

_____

_____

KEEPING COMPANY WITH GOD

(Optional Reading: "Tuning In," pages 286–287)

Because prayer is a relationship and not a transaction, I do not pray in order to win God over to my will—quite the opposite. As I pray, increasingly I realize that my prayers do not rise out of but flow through me. Instead of trying to win God over, God has won me; my use of God's identity and name shows that. Keeping company with God, I sense in my requests the timbre of an echo, God's voice entering softly and bouncing back to its source. So many of the concerns I bring to God in prayer, I realize, have their origin in God's own self, who implanted those concerns in me.

What are some possible ways in which you might listen for "the echo of God's voice" in your own prayers?

_____

_____

_____

_____

_____

_____

_____

_____

_____

_____

_____

_____

_____

_____

_____

_____

_____

Unlike mastering a foreign language, my prayers do not grow more articulate as I learn new words and lofty expressions. If anything, prayer involves *unlearning* the seductions of pride and self-assertion I battle each day. I advance only as I fall backwards, in humble dependence, on the One who called me into being.

What have you had to "unlearn" in prayer?

PRAYER'S GREATEST TRIUMPH MAY NOT BE HEALING OR DELIVERANCE, BUT THE ABILITY TO COURAGEOUSLY ACCEPT THE TERMS OF LIFE WE HAVE BEEN HANDED, WHATEVER THEY BE.

Here I am! I stand at the door and knock. If anyone hears my voice and open the door, I will come in and eat with him, and he with me.

Revelation 3:2

Choose one of the multiple images in this verse — for example, "Here I am!" ... "I stand at the door and knock" ... "if anyone hears my voice" ... "if anyone ... opens the door" ... "I will come in" ... "and eat with him" ... "and he with me." Use that one image as a prayer springboard, a way of focusing a short time of "conversation" with God. If it helps, consider writing your way into this conversation.

_____

_____

_____

_____

_____

_____

_____

_____

_____

_____

_____

_____

_____

_____

_____

_____

_____

_____

_____

What, if anything, is changing or developing in your understanding of what it means for you to "keep company" with God?

_____

_____

_____

_____

_____

_____

_____

_____

_____

_____

_____

_____

_____

_____

_____

> THE SAME JESUS WHO SPOKE OF FAITH AS A MUSTARD SEED ALSO GAVE US THE STORY ABOUT A WIDOW WEARING DOWN A JUDGE WITH HER PERSISTENCE.

_____

_____

_____

_____

The Pharisees had excellent prayer lives as judged by eloquence and regularity, yet Jesus condemned their showy spirituality because it did not translate into real life. God was on their lips, but far from their hearts.

Do you ever find yourself in danger of praying like the Pharisees? When does it typically happen?

_____

_____

_____

_____

_____

_____

_____

_____

_____

_____

_____

_____

_____

_____

_____

_____

_____

_____

_____

_____

ike a farmer, I have known good years and bad years with prayer, seasons of
ontentment and gratitude and seasons of anguish and dereliction. I expected
straight-line vector of growth, something like the Wall Street charts of
iutual funds that steadily gain in value ever year. Instead, the line veers up
nd down erratically like that on a heart monitor. Only later, in retrospect, can
see that the darkest times solidified my faith and that somehow the words I
rote in those times God used to speak to others.

Vhat factors or circumstances, if you can point to them, tend to drive your
ps and downs in prayer?

> NONE OF US CAN AVOID
> SUFFERING, BUT WE CAN
> GAIN FROM IT QUALITIES
> LIKE PATIENCE, SYMPATHY,
> INSIGHT, SELF-SURRENDER,
> AND PRESENT THESE BACK AS
> AN OFFERING TO GOD.

QUESTIONING

I believe in prayer and its power to change both people and events. Nevertheless, when I hear a person describe a remarkable escape from an airplane crash, I cannot help thinking about the people who died in the same crash, many of them praying just as fervently.

What makes the difference? Why does God appear to be so unpredictable and arbitrary in responding to our prayers? I know many situations in which pray-ers claim to receive assurance from God that a sick person will be healed—only to see that person die. Questions inevitably stir up on what we believe God is like, whether we should keep praying in spite of our uncertainties and unbelief, and what might happen within us in the very process of wrestling with unanswered prayer.

Perhaps one of the greatest reasons to face into those questions, rather than ignore or suppress them, is to keep our prayers alive. If our hearts grow dead to questions, then they will likely grow indifferent to prayer. Two-thirds of the psalms, in the Bible's model prayer book, are laments—a beautiful model of pray-ers pouring out their hearts to God about their disappointments and confusion. Why does God not answer? Why so much pain and injustice in the world?

It has helped me to look at God's unpredictability as one more manifestation of the reality that God is a person—not a principle, not a philosophy, not a logical necessity. God's character is faithful and dependable, but God's actions are neither predictable nor subject to our control. God's ways are different than our ways. Prayer is a crucible in which we are privileged to glimpse these differences in ways that leave us hungering for more.

(Optional Reading: Chapter 15 opening, "The Sound of Silence," pages 198–199)

What are some of your most nagging questions about prayer—not the hypo-thetical, "what-if" kind, but the ones that leave you troubled and uncertain about how to pray for real people in particular circumstances?

_____

_____

_____

_____

_____

_____

_____

_____

_____

_____

_____

_____

_____

_____

_____

_____

_____

_____

_____

_____

_____

_____

(Optional Reading: "The Questions Beneath," pages 204–205)

We know in part, and we prophesy in part, but when perfection comes, the imperfect disappears. Now we see but a poor reflection as in a mirror; then we shall see face to face. Now I know in part; then I shall know fully, even as I am fully known.

1 Corinthians 13:9–10, 12

Think about the concerns, worries, and opportunities of one day in your life— today—and write them down as they come to mind. Is there any one of them that you would look at differently, or pray about differently, in the light of this perspective from Paul's first letter to the Corinthians?

_____

_____

_____

_____

_____

_____

_____

_____

_____

_____

_____

_____

_____

_____

_____

_____

_____

_____

have learned, when confronted with urgent questions, always to begin with
esus, the fullest revelation of God on earth.

Consider one or two of your most nagging questions about God's ways in
our life, in the lives of your loved ones, or in the crises of the world today.
f you were able to pose these questions directly to Jesus, face to face, what
vould you want to say to him?

_____

_____

_____

_____

_____

_____

_____

_____

_____

_____

_____

_____

_____

_____

_____

_____

_____

> UNANSWERED PRAYER
> BRINGS ME FACE-TO-FACE
> WITH THE MYSTERY THAT
> SILENCED PAUL: THE
> PROFOUND DIFFERENCE
> BETWEEN MY PERSPECTIVE
> AND GOD'S.

_____

_____

_____

_____

_____

_____

The question nags at me: How does this most internal and private act, prayer, result in motion that contributes to the reign of God in the world? I examine myself first of all. When I studied the Sermon on the Mount, I made a list of some of its commands: Store up treasures in heaven, not earth. Love your enemies. Give to the one who asks you. Reading the words of Jesus is listening to God at its most basic, and most discomfiting, level. Each week I go over that list. Am I a peacemaker? Where am I storing treasure? Do I stand up for justice? Do I lift the humble and oppose the proud, as Jesus did?

In what areas of your life are you most likely to see a gap between what you pray for and how you live? Consider this thoughtfully, as a positive opportunity for taking one step toward change, rather than harshly, as a reason to punish yourself with guilt.

_____

_____

_____

_____

_____

_____

| "IF YOU WANT TO SEE |
| GOD SMILE, TELL HIM |
| YOUR PLANS," GOES AN |
| OLD SAYING. |

_____

_____

_____

_____

_____

_____

(Optional Reading: "Heart Desire," pages 267–268)

A man with leprosy came to him and begged him on his knees, "If you are willing, you can make me clean."

Filled with compassion, Jesus reached out his hand and touched the man. "I am willing," he said. "Be clean!" Immediately the leprosy left him and he was cured.

Mark 1:40–42

What kinds of thoughts do you have in response to this account of healing?

_____

_____

_____

_____

_____

_____

_____

_____

_____

_____

_____

_____

_____

_____

_____

_____

_____

_____

_____

_____

Already in this journal you have listed some of your most important questions about prayer. How do they affect the way you (do or don't) pray?

_____

_____

_____

_____

_____

> MY OWN CONCERN ABOUT INAPPROPRIATE OR IRRELEVANT PRAYERS MELTS AWAY AS I VIEW PRAYER LESS AS A TECHNIQUE THAN AS A RELATIONSHIP, A WAY OF KEEPING COMPANY WITH GOD.

_____

_____

_____

_____

_____

_____

_____

_____

_____

_____

_____

_____

_____

_____

(Optional Reading: "God's Presence," pages 273–274)

Sometimes when I bring requests to God, I can't even envision a pleasing outcome. I simply bring my concern, my compassion, and present it to One who cares more than I.

Do you struggle with any prayer requests that seem futile to pray about?

_____

_____

_____

_____

_____

_____

_____

_____

_____

_____

_____

_____

_____

_____

_____

_____

_____

_____

_____

_____

"Do not be anxious about anything," counsels the apostle Paul, "but in everything, by prayer and petition, with thanksgiving, present your requests to God. And the peace of God, which transcends all understanding, will guard your hearts and your minds in Christ Jesus." One translator renders that last sentence, "And the peace which God himself has will, beyond anything we can intellectually grasp, stand guard over your hearts and minds, which are within the reality of Jesus the anointed." Faith does not necessarily remove the difficulties that prompt anxiety—Paul, after all, wrote those words from a Roman prison—but connects us to an unseen reality that enfolds them.

What in your life seems so anxiety-producing that you have trouble presenting it to God in prayer? If you simply write it down and sit with it, silently, for a few minutes, that act alone could be a first step of bringing it to God in prayer.

> PRAYER IS A STATE AS MUCH AS AN ACT, A FACT THAT EASILY GETS FORGOTTEN WHEN WE CONFINE IT TO ONE OR TWO ISOLATED INSTANCES A DAY.

My heart is not proud, O LORD,
    my eyes are not haughty;
I do not concern myself with great matters
    or things too wonderful for me.
But I have stilled and quieted my soul;
    like a weaned child with its mother,
    like a weaned child is my soul within me.
O Israel, put your hope in the LORD
    both now and forevermore.

Psalm 131

Read this passage slowly and thoughtfully, allowing it to sink down into your mind and heart. What words or images stand out to you?

_____

_____

_____

_____

_____

_____

_____

_____

_____

_____

_____

_____

_____

_____

_____

_____

The Bible speaks in a language relevant to its own day, and I imagine if John were writing Revelation today he would speak not of fire and streets paved with gold but of black holes, the reversible arrows of time, eleven dimensions, and alternate universes. If so, no doubt the astronomers and particle physicists would be the ones bowing in awe.

To most moderns, however, a sense of awe comes with great difficulty. We have domesticated angels into stuffed toys and Christmas ornaments, made cartoons of St. Peter at the gate of heaven, tamed the phenomenon of Easter with bunny rabbits, and substituted for the awe of shepherds and wise men cute elves and a jolly man dressed in red. Almighty God gets nicknamed "The Big Guy" and "The Man Upstairs."

How do you think your prayers would change if the veil was temporarily pulled aside and you could glimpse the startling reality of an infinite God?

_____

_____

_____

_____

_____

_____

_____

_____

_____

_____

_____

_____

_____

_____

_____

_____

_____

Choose a longstanding desire or prayer request that you have brought to God in the past. Are you learning anything about God that makes you feel hopeful in praying about this again? If not, what are the obstacles to hope?

_____

_____

_____

_____

_____

_____

_____

_____

_____

_____

_____

_____

_____

_____

_____

_____

> OUR PRAYERS ARE LIKE
> HAMMER-BLOWS AGAINST
> A STONE WALL—AGAINST
> THE GATES OF HELL, TO
> BORROW JESUS' IMAGE,
> AND THOSE GATES WILL
> NOT PREVAIL.

_____

_____

_____

_____

_____

_____

I accept that doubt will occasionally invade my practice of prayer. I speak of my doubt openly with God rather than trying to deny or hide it. For validation I turn to the expressions of doubt in the Bible and make them my prayers. For insight I consider my doubts in the light of Jesus. And for survival I cling to the faith of others. I pray with the tiniest morsel of faith I can summon up, recognizing that the act of prayer itself is a giant step of faith.

Do you know anyone who has given up praying for something because he or she doubted that God would answer? Is there any way you can help, directly or indirectly?

_____

_____

_____

_____

_____

_____

_____

_____

_____

_____

_____

_____

_____

_____

_____

_____

_____

As a father has compassion on his children,
    so the LORD has compassion on those who fear him;
For he knows how we are formed,
    he remembers that we are dust.

Psalm 103:13–14

What does this passage tell you about God? How might it affect your prayers?

_____

_____

_____

_____

_____

_____

_____

_____

_____

_____

_____

_____

> NO MESSAGE COMES THROUGH MORE FORCEFULLY IN THE BIBLE THAN THAT THE HUMAN SPECIES MATTERS PROFOUNDLY TO GOD.

_____

_____

_____

_____

_____

_____

Many psalms begin with praise and end with request, as if the litany of what God has done in the past offers evidence as to what God may do in the future.

What has God done in your past that can give you a grateful and hopeful heart as you face the future?

_____

_____

_____

_____

_____

_____

> FOR A TIME, GOD HAS CHOSEN TO OPERATE ON THIS BROKEN PLANET MOSTLY FROM THE BOTTOM UP RATHER THAN FROM THE TOP DOWN — A PATTERN GOD'S OWN SON SUBJECTED HIMSELF TO WHILE ON EARTH.

_____

_____

_____

_____

_____

_____

_____

_____

_____

_____

_____

_____

_____

_____

_____

_____

Vhen I wonder if God cares, and question why God tolerates a world so full f evil and suffering, I look at Jesus and learn from his example to trust a wing Father despite all appearances. When even that fails, I look for evidence f God in the lives of others. Like the disciple Thomas (see John 20:24–31), I urround myself with the faith of others when mine falters.

lave you ever been helped by others during times when prayer has been espe- ially difficult for you? List all the instances that come to mind. Now reverse oles: What can you offer to others?

_____

_____

_____

_____

_____

_____

_____

_____

_____

_____

_____

_____

_____

_____

_____

_____

_____

_____

_____

_____

What needs and desires most often drive you to prayer in this season of your life

> PRAYER INVITES US
> TO REST IN THE FACT
> THAT GOD IS IN
> CONTROL, AND THE
> WORLD'S PROBLEMS
> ARE ULTIMATELY
> GOD'S, NOT OURS.

(Optional Reading: "Am I prepared for the possibility . . . ?" pages 264–266)

The LORD is my shepherd, I shall not be in want.
>   He makes me lie down in green pastures,
he leads me beside quiet waters,
>   he restores my soul.

Psalm 23:1–3

These images stir great longing in us. Have you ever felt the way the psalmist describes? How did God make it possible for you to feel comforted?

_____

_____

_____

_____

_____

_____

_____

_____

_____

_____

_____

_____

_____

_____

_____

_____

_____

_____

_____

(Optional Reading: "Grace," pages 279–280)

In one of his letters, Paul described himself as afflicted but not crushed, perplexed but not driven to despair, persecuted but not forsaken, struck down but not destroyed (1 Corinthians 4:8–9). He learned a different level of faith, one that does not remove difficulty but nevertheless withstands, a fidelity in which weakness transforms into strength and prayers for healing melt into prayers of acceptance.

Where are you facing difficulties that seem unlikely to be removed or relieved? What would divine strength look like in the midst of such circumstances?

_____

_____

_____

_____

_____

_____

_____

_____

_____

_____

_____

_____

_____

_____

_____

_____

_____

_____

_____

An over-emphasis on requests, especially those that are denied, distorts the central meaning of prayer. We are not trying to talk a reluctant God into doing something but rather seeking to get into the stream of God's love, God's will in this world.

How might your practice of prayer be enriched by shifting focus—instead of asking God for something you care about, requesting that God give *you* to some cause or someone God cares about?

GOD, WHO MADE SPACE
IN THE MOST LITERAL
SENSE, THE UNIVERSE,
NEEDS US TO PROTECT
A GOD-SPACE, TO
PREVENT OUR LIVES
FROM FILLING UP WITH
OTHER THINGS.

When God finally spoke into the anguished vacuum of Job's unanswered questions, the discussion at hand was radically redirected from cause-and-effect hypotheses to the vast power and creativity of God. Overcome with awe, Job replied, "Surely I spoke of things I did not understand, things too wonderful for me to know." (Job 42:3)

How would you describe the difference between presumptuous demands for answers and honest questions? As an example, choose one prayer and phrase it two different ways: first as a demand for an answer, and second as an honest question.

_____

_____

_____

_____

_____

_____

_____

_____

_____

_____

_____

_____

_____

_____

_____

_____

_____

_____

(Optional Reading: "Do I wrongly blame God ... ?" pages 262–264)

Since some of Paul's most thanksgiving-saturated letters were written from prison, it seems clear that thanksgiving can emerge from unlikely circumstances. Indeed, from my visits to countries where Christians live under suffering or persecution I have almost concluded that, paradoxically, hardship may be more likely to produce thanksgiving.

Can you point to struggles in your life that have deepened your gratitude to God? How did thankfulness emerge from them?

_____

_____

_____

_____

_____

_____

_____

_____

_____

_____

_____

_____

_____

_____

_____

_____

_____

> WITH PRAYER MUCH OF THE BENEFIT TAKES PLACE BEHIND THE SCENES, BENEATH THE LEVEL OF CONSCIOUS AWARENESS, IN WAYS DIFFICULT TO MEASURE.

_____

_____

_____

_____

KEEPING COMPANY WITH GOD

(Optional Reading: "Available," pages 276–277)

The apostle Peter, who was later martyred, wrote to a suffering church, "In this you greatly rejoice, though now for a little while you may have had to suffer grief in all kinds of trials. These have come so that your faith—of greater worth than gold, which perishes even though refined by fire—may be proved genuine and may result in praise, glory and honor when Jesus Christ is revealed" (1 Peter 1:6–7). Peter knew both ways to bring God glory: the heady way of supernatural healings, prison escapes, and important leadership roles as well as the upside-down way of prison and crucifixion.

Suffering draws some people closer to God and leaves others bitter and resentful toward God. What do you think makes the difference?

_____

_____

_____

_____

_____

_____

> NOT EVERYONE WILL REACH SUCH AN EXALTED PLATEAU OF ACCEPTANCE. SOMETIMES WE NEVER ATTAIN THE FAITH FOR WHICH WE STRIVE. AND THAT IS WHY WE PRAY.

_____

_____

_____

_____

_____

_____

_____

_____

_____

_____

By definition no one deserves grace and yet it descends, dropping "as the gentle rain from heaven," to borrow Shakespeare's comments about mercy (*The Merchant of Venice*, Act 4.1, line 183). In response, human spirits ascend beyond heights they could ever achieve on their own.

To someone who had never experienced God's grace in the midst of life's difficult or confusing circumstances, how would you describe it?

_____

_____

_____

_____

_____

_____

_____

_____

_____

_____

_____

_____

_____

_____

_____

_____

_____

_____

DEEPENING

Our age conditions us to seek self-improvement by managing more information more efficiently, consulting success gurus, spending more on higher upgrades, buying more than we need to make sure we have everything we want. Naturally, then, we are tempted to view prayer as a task to complete, a skill to parse into steps of proficiency, a lifestyle component to help us become well-rounded. We like to be in control, and that kind of approach to prayer would make it manageable.

But prayer is ultimately a mystery—and by definition, therefore, beyond our control and thus unmanageable. If the apostle Paul were asked to sum up what is necessary for growing in prayer, perhaps he would have answered with his concluding counsel in one letter: "pray continually" (1 Thessalonians 5:17).

Author John Sanford describes an old well that stood outside the front door of a family farmhouse in New Hampshire, a bright spot in his memories of summer vacations. As years passed, the farmhouse got modernized. No longer needed, the old well was sealed for use in possible future emergencies.

As an adult, Sanford found himself hankering for the cold, pure water of his youth. So one day he returned to the farmhouse, unsealed the well, and lowered a bucket for a nostalgic taste of the delightful refreshment he remembered. When he hoisted the bucket, he discovered that the well had now gone bone dry. Perplexed, he began to question the locals, who informed him that wells of that sort are fed by hundreds of tiny underground rivulets seeping a steady flow of water. As long as water is drawn out of the well, new water will flow in through the rivulets. But when the water stops flowing, the rivulets clog with mud. The well had gone dry not because it was used too much, but because it wasn't used enough.

Sanford observed that our souls are like that well. The eventual consequence for not drinking deeply of God is losing the ability to drink at all. Prayerlessness is its own punishment, both its disease and its cause.* To deepen your prayer life, keep praying.

*John A. Sanford, *The Kingdom Within* (Philadelphia and New York: J. P. Lippincott Company, 1970), 15–16.

What have you found most helpful in keeping the waters of prayer flowing in your life? What tends to dry them up?

(Optional Reading: Chapter 22 opening, "Prayer and God," pages 314–315)

Pray in the Spirit on all occasions with all kinds of prayers and requests.

Ephesians 6:18

Praying "constantly" amid all the demands and distractions of life is no easy matter. What are some practical ways of doing what Paul urges in this passage?

_____

_____

_____

_____

_____

_____

_____

_____

_____

_____

_____

_____

_____

_____

_____

_____

_____

_____

_____

_____

_____

_____

We are assured that God lives inside us: "the kingdom of God is within you," Jesus said (Luke 17:21). God's Spirit indwells, so that God is present in everything I do today, every person I meet. I need only acknowledge that presence.

Have you ever thought of prayer as simply a way of acknowledging God's presence? What would such a prayer look or sound like for you?

_____

_____

_____

_____

_____

_____

_____

_____

_____

_____

_____

_____

_____

_____

| A CHILD DOES NOT DECIDE, "I THINK I WILL IMITATE DAD." HE ABSORBS FAMILY TRAITS UNCONSCIOUSLY, BY SUSTAINED CONTACT. |

_____

_____

_____

_____

_____

_____

_____

_____

_____

_____

_____

Learning to pray is like learning a language, and Psalms is a great tutor. Some people look for psalms that fit their moods. If they're angry or depressed, they look for a psalm to articulate that feeling. I approach them differently. I let the psalm determine the mood. It's good practice, I think, to pray things that have nothing to do with my mood.

As a result, the psalms are training me. When I hit the difficult, cursing psalms, I think of present-day parallels: suicide bombers, North Korea, modern genocide. When I come across psalms that speak deeply to me, I try memorizing portions. Gradually, I've learned to sense God's presence through the images and the daily rhythm expressed in the psalms.

Choose a favorite psalm—and read through it, out loud. If you have never "prayed the psalms" before, consider experimenting for a week, reading one psalm each morning or evening (or both) as your prayer, in the words God has provided. What strikes you?

f I speak in the tongues of men and of angels, but have not love, I am only a resounding gong or a clanging cymbal. If I have the gift of prophecy and can athom all mysteries and all knowledge, and if I have a faith that can move nountains, but have not love, I am nothing. If I give all I possess to the poor and surrender my body to the flames, but have not love, I gain nothing.

1 Corinthians 13:1–3

Try rewriting this passage in your own words, refocusing it on prayer in place of the other spiritual activities — such as "the tongue of men and of angels" and "the gift of prophecy." How can we pray *with love?*

_____

_____

_____

_____

_____

_____

_____

_____

_____

_____

_____

_____

_____

_____

_____

> PRAYER ALLOWS ME TO
> SEE OTHERS AS GOD
> SEES THEM (AND ME):
> UNIQUELY FLAWED
> AND UNIQUELY GIFTED
> BEARERS OF GOD'S
> IMAGE.

_____

_____

_____

_____

In Moses' farewell speech to the Israelites before they crossed into the Promised Land, he told them to "love the LORD your God, listen to his voice, and hold fast to him" (Deuteronomy 30:20). What does it mean to "listen to God's voice"? Think through your day. What might encourage such a time of listening? What works against it?

_____

_____

_____

_____

_____

> BY NATURE I RESIST TECHNIQUES, ESPECIALLY THOSE RELATED TO SPIRITUAL DISCIPLINES. I WOULD PREFER TO KEEP MY RELATIONSHIP WITH GOD IMPROMPTU. THE PROBLEM IS, EVERY TIME I PROCEED DOWN SUCH AN IDEALISTIC PATH GOD GETS PUSHED TO THE SIDE.

_____

_____

_____

_____

_____

_____

am learning the difference between saying prayers, which is an activity, and praying, which is a soul attitude, a "lifting up of the mind to God." Praying in that sense can transform every task, from shoveling snow to defragmenting a computer's hard drive.

Can you think of times in your life when prayer seems not so much "an activity" as a "soul attitude"? What does that look like?

_____

_____

_____

_____

_____

_____

_____

_____

_____

_____

_____

_____

_____

_____

_____

_____

_____

_____

_____

_____

_____

_____

If you spend any time with Christians in Asian countries, you will quickly discover their intense commitment to praying together. In Korea, for example tens of thousands of people stay up each Friday night praying, many sitting in a retreat center called "Prayer Mountain." When Asian Christians visit the West, they are often surprised to encounter churches with several thousand attendees that have no scheduled times of corporate prayer—or, if they do, the meetings are sparsely attended and void of life. Although church leaders have superb training in accessories to worship (musical groups, Power Point presentations, drama teams), scant attention is paid to the role of prayer in worship. By contrast, in places where Christians are persecuted, prayer meetings keep the church alive.

Recall some of your experiences of praying with others (such as in a worship or prayer service, with a small group, or perhaps just with friends). What do you think are some critical factors that make a difference between a positive o a negative experience of corporate prayer?

_____

_____

_____

_____

_____

_____

_____

_____

_____

_____

_____

_____

_____

_____

_____

(Optional Reading: Chapter 11 opening, "Ask, Seek, Knock," pages 145–146)

Jesus said, "Ask and it will be given to you; seek and you will find; knock and the door will be opened to you. For everyone who asks receives; he who seeks finds; and to him who knocks, the door will be opened.

"Which of you, if his son asks for bread, will give him a stone? Or if he asks for a fish, will give him a snake? If you, then, though you are evil, know how to give good gifts to your children, how much more will your Father in heaven give good gifts to those who ask him! So in everything, do to others what you would have them do to you, for this sums up the Law and the Prophets."

Matthew 7:7–12

Read this passage slowly and thoughtfully, allowing it to sink down into your mind and heart. What words or images stand out to you?

_____

_____

_____

_____

_____

_____

_____

_____

_____

> AT ITS BEST, PRAYER DOES NOT SEEK TO MANIPULATE GOD INTO DOING MY WILL—QUITE THE OPPOSITE. PRAYER ENTERS THE POOL OF GOD'S LOVE AND WIDENS OUTWARD.

_____

_____

_____

We often think of prayer as an act of emotion rather than mind, but a prayer based on feelings becomes dangerously vulnerable to shifts in mood. Every lover knows that love involves a mutual education. Passion may draw two people together, but it takes a studied attention to the other's needs and desires to forge a love that lasts.

What, for you, are some of the most important ways of attending to your relationship with God?

_____

_____

_____

_____

_____

_____

_____

_____

_____

_____

_____

_____

_____

_____

_____

_____

_____

_____

_____

n a culture that values accomplishment, we tend to think of prayer as a task we need to do, rather than as an opportunity simply to be with God. What are you learning about prayer as a way of "tuning in" to God or resting in God's presence?

_____

_____

_____

_____

_____

_____

_____

_____

_____

_____

_____

_____

_____

_____

_____

> LOVE GOD WITH ALL YOUR HEART, JESUS SAID. LISTEN TO YOUR LIFE: TO ITS PASSION, ITS DREAMS AND DISAPPOINTMENTS, ITS TEDIUM AS WELL AS ITS DRAMA. IT CAME TO YOU AS A GIFT AND EACH DAY, TOO, UNRAVELS AS A GIFT. GOD WANTS AN INVITATION TO SHARE IN ITS EVERY DETAIL.

_____

_____

_____

_____

_____

_____

_____

_____

Occasionally I hear something like this said after a great service of worship: "That was wonderful! Too bad we have to go back to the real world now." The assumption seems to be that what happened in worship was a pleasant and therapeutic diversion, and that the real challenge is out there in the rough-and-tumble world. Doesn't that confuse substance with its shadow? To the believer, what was seen and felt in worship *is* the real thing.

From the perspective of heaven, prayer is the real work on earth, the thin line of connection between two worlds: one of distorted reality and one of true reality. Our life on earth here is a kind of constructed, virtual reality. "Behind the curtain" lies the real world, of which we see only glimpses.

In what ways, if any, do you experience prayer as a way of glimpsing, or connecting with, the spiritual world "behind the curtain" of the ordinary?

Praise be to the God and Father of our Lord Jesus Christ, the Father of compassion and the God of all comfort, who comforts us in all our troubles, so that we can comfort those in any trouble with the comfort we ourselves have received from God. For just as the sufferings of Christ flow over into our lives, so also through Christ our comfort overflows.

2 Corinthians 1:3–5

Think of someone in your church or community—perhaps yourself—who has gone through a difficult time of suffering. Did other Christians present a "God of all comfort"? What can believers do in reaching out to those who suffer in ways that offer comfort rather than confusion?

_____

_____

_____

_____

_____

_____

_____

> WRITTEN PRAYERS SERVE AN ESPECIALLY USEFUL PURPOSE, I HAVE FOUND, DURING PERIODS OF SPIRITUAL DRYNESS, WHEN SPONTANEOUS PRAYER SEEMS AN IMPOSSIBLE CHORE. I BORROW THE WORDS, IF NOT THE FAITH, OF OTHERS WHEN MY OWN WORDS FAIL.

_____

_____

_____

All the main New Testament passages on suffering emphasize that God can redeem hardship so that it produces present benefits—patience, perseverance, character, maturity, hope—as well as future glory (see Romans 5:1–5). Seen from the longer view, hardships are growing pains toward a future perfection. We want comfort and security and insulation from others' problems. Jesus calls us to compassion and struggle and active involvement in the suffering of others. The path we resist turns out to be the path we need.

What role has prayer played in the way you have handled suffering? Choose one experience as an example, and write about it—for example, when you were or weren't able to pray; whether you were aware of others praying for you; whether or not prayer seemed to affect circumstances; whether God seemed present or absent.

_____

_____

_____

_____

_____

_____

_____

_____

> THE INCLUSION OF SO MANY
> UNANSWERED PRAYERS IN
> THE BIBLE MAKES GOD ALL
> THE MORE TRUSTWORTHY.

_____

_____

_____

_____

_____

_____

A few years ago a prominent charismatic church leader in the U.K., David Watson, was battling cancer. He spoke often in radio broadcasts of the encouragement he had received from believers around the world who promised him, "This sickness is not unto death." The illness turned out to be fatal, though, and those same Christians had to come to terms with their misguided encouragement and, in some cases, shattered faith. J. I. Packer wrote the foreword to *Fear No Evil*, in which Watson bared his soul about his own doubts and struggles. As Packer said, "David's theology led him to believe, right to the end, that God wanted to heal his body. Mine leads me rather to say that God evidently wanted David home, and healed his whole person by taking him to glory in the way that he will one day heal us all. Health and life, I would say, in the full and final sense of those words, are not what we die *out of*, but what we die *into*."*

What has been your experience in prayers for those battling a progressively fatal illness, or recovery from a near-fatal injury? In what ways, if any, has that experience affected the way you are likely to pray for someone in similar circumstances?

_____

_____

_____

_____

_____

_____

_____

_____

_____

_____

_____

*J. I. Packer, "Foreword," in *Fear No Evil*, by David C. K. Watson (Carol Stream, IL: Harold Shaw Publishers, 1985), p. 7.

Describe some of the ways in which attending to the presence of God in your day-to-day life can help you become more aware of the needs of others — for example, praying for someone could prompt you to make a phone call or write a note ... asking for a sense of God's presence might prompt you about a friend who needs to feel God's presence through you ... confessing sin might remind you to pray blessing upon someone who has sinned against you ... taking your heartache to God over a loved one in crisis could galvanize you to give money or volunteer service to an organization reaching out to others in similar difficulties ... worshiping God with others could remind you of the shut-ins who can't join you and need a visitor.

_____

_____

_____

_____

_____

_____

_____

_____

_____

_____

> IF PRAYER IS MY RESPONSE TO GOD'S PRESENCE, FIRST I MUST TUNE IN TO THAT PRESENCE.

_____

_____

_____

_____

_____

_____

_____

_____

Jesus told this parable about prayer: "Two men went up to the temple to pray, one a Pharisee and the other a tax collector. The Pharisee stood up and prayed about himself: 'God, I thank you that I am not like other men — robbers, evildoers, adulterers — or even like this tax collector. I fast twice a week and give a tenth of all I get.'

"But the tax collector stood at a distance. He would not even look up to heaven, but beat his breast and said, 'God, have mercy on me, a sinner.' "I tell you that this man, rather than the other, went home justified before God. For everyone who exalts himself will be humbled, and he who humbles himself will be exalted."

Luke 18:10–14

About all these two men have in common is that both are addressing God in prayer. List the differences between them — what was the focus of each man's prayer? How would you describe each one's self-image and God-image (i.e., his view of God)?

_____

_____

_____

_____

_____

_____

_____

_____

_____

_____

_____

_____

_____

Reading the psalms, I realize how impoverished is my practice of praise. The psalmists longed to "gaze upon the beauty of the LORD" (27:4), panted for God as a deer pants after water (42:1), preferred spending one day in God's presence than a thousand years elsewhere (84:10). For many moderns the act of worship—whether delivering the kids to Sunday School or attending church on religious holidays such as Christmas and Easter—is something to get through before resuming normal life. To the Hebrews, worship was the goal, not something you get over with. They had an appetite for God.

List some of the times when you are most likely to feel your heart stirred with praise and thanksgiving. How does your praise for God express itself during those times?

_____

_____

_____

_____

_____

_____

_____

_____

_____

_____

_____

_____

_____

_____

_____

_____

_____

_____

_____

Most parents feel a pang when their child outgrows dependence, even while knowing the growth to be healthy and normal. With God, the rules change. I never outgrow dependence, and to the extent I think I do, I delude myself. Asking for help lies at the root of prayer: the Lord's Prayer itself consists of a string of such requests. Prayer is a declaration of dependence upon God.

Think about the ways in which you have grown and changed over the years because of prayer. What in your life has been strongly influenced by your experience with prayer? Another way to ask this might be, How has the way you pray changed the way you live?

_____

_____

_____

_____

_____

_____

_____

_____

_____

_____

_____

_____

_____

_____

> THOUGH NOT SOLVING ALL THE PROBLEMS ON EARTH, JESUS' MIRACLES DID GIVE A CLEAR SIGN OF HOW THE WORLD SHOULD BE, AND SOMEDAY WILL BE.

_____

_____

Jesus said, "This, then, is how you should pray:

"'Our Father in heaven,
hallowed be your name,
your kingdom come,
your will be done
    on earth as it is in heaven.
Give us today our daily bread.
Forgive us our debts,
    as we also have forgiven our debtors.
And lead us not into temptation,
but deliver us from the evil one.'"

Matthew 6:9–13

How would you identify what Jesus considered important about the way we pray, based upon this teaching? As part of your reflection, pray this prayer out loud, listening for the echo of God's voice in the words Jesus gave us.

_____

_____

_____

_____

_____

_____

_____

_____

_____

_____

_____

_____

_____

The practice of prayer raises so many questions for us that we tend to focus on the unknowns. What, for you, are the most important things you do know, or believe, about prayer?

> I PRAY IN TRUST THAT THE ACT OF PRAYER IS GOD'S DESIGNATED WAY OF CLOSING THE VAST GULF BETWEEN INFINITY AND ME.

Jesus' final words at the end of Revelation are "I am coming soon," followed by an urgent, resounding prayer, "Amen. Come, Lord Jesus" (Revelation 22:20). That prayer remains unanswered in an era of history perilously suspended between his first appearance, as a baby in a manger, and his second, as the one with blazing eyes described in Revelation.

How does the promise of Jesus' return shape your understanding of partnership in his work on earth now, if at all? What about the world would you like to see changed by Jesus?

_____

_____

_____

_____

_____

_____

_____

_____

_____

_____

_____

_____

_____

_____

_____

_____

_____

_____

I am astonished that God uses anything of me, including my prayer, to accomplish anything of worth on this earth. That is God's choice, once more a choice that dignifies us even as it respects our freedom.

God does not force us to love him. How do you see prayer a way of expressing your free choice to love God?

_____

_____

_____

_____

_____

_____

_____

_____

_____

_____

_____

| JESUS SET THE |
| PATTERN FOR PRAYER |
| AS A CONTINUOUS MODE |
| OF FRIENDSHIP. |

_____

_____

_____

_____

_____

_____

(Optional Reading: "Resuming the Conversation," pages 325–328)

I pray in astonished belief that God desires an ongoing relationship. I pray in trust that the act of prayer is God's designated way of closing the vast gulf between infinity and me. I pray in order to put myself in the stream of God's healing work on earth. I pray as I breathe—because I can't help it.

How would you complete the following sentences?

"I want to pray because _____

_____

_____

_____

_____

_____

_____ ."

"I pray in order to _____

_____

_____

_____

_____

_____

_____ ."

"I would like to deepen my experience of prayer by _____

_____

_____

_____

_____

_____

_____

_____

_____ ."

We want to hear from you. Please send your comments about this book to us in care of zreview@zondervan.com. Thank you.

ZONDERVAN.com/
AUTHORTRACKER
follow your favorite authors

Prayer

Does It Make Any Difference?

Philip Yancey, Author of
What's So Amazing About Grace?

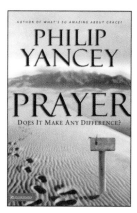

In his most powerful book since *What's So Amazing About Grace?* and *The Jesus I Never Knew*, Philip Yancey probes the very heartbeat—the most fundamental, challenging, perplexing, and deeply rewarding aspect—of our relationship with God: prayer. What is prayer? How does it work? And more importantly, does it work? In theory, prayer is the essential human act, a priceless point of contact between us and the God of the universe. In practice, prayer is often frustrating, confusing, and fraught with mystery. *Prayer: Does It Make Any Difference?* is an exploration of the mysterious intersection where God and humans meet and relate. Writing as a fellow pilgrim, Yancey explores such questions as:

- Is God listening?
- Why should God care about me?
- If God knows everything, what's the point of prayer?
- Why do answers to prayer seem so inconsistent and capricious?
- Why does God seem sometimes close and sometimes far away?
- How can I make prayer more satisfying?

"I have found that the most important purpose of prayer may be to let ourselves be loved by God," says Yancey. *Prayer: Does It Make Any Difference?* encourages us to pray to God the Father who sees what lies ahead of us, knows what lies within us, and who invites us into an eternal partnership-through prayer. Also available: unabridged audio CD.

Hardcover, Jacketed: 0-310-27105-3

Pick up a copy today at your favorite bookstore!